C0-DKL-133

TALKING DOGS

VOLUME 1

CELESTA LETCHWORTH

AT CHRISTMAS

TALKING DOGS AT CHRISTMAS, Volume 1: Hilarious Holiday Dog Photos with Captions
Copyright © 2022 by Celesta Letchworth.

ISBN: 978-1-947566-28-6

Published by Fermata House: Versailles, Kentucky www.fermatahouse.com

All photo acknowledgements/credits with links are available at www.fermatahouse.com

Dedicated to Molly.
You made a dog-lover out of me.
See ya on the flip side, Girl.

Do these antlers

make my butt look big?

Why does Gerald
get to wear the wreath
and I'm stuck with
the tiny hat?!

Never fails.
Always.
The tiny.
Hat.

DOG-IN-A-BAG

Just add water

and watch him grow!

The next snowball
has your name on it.

And it's gonna be yellow.

I hate it when I have to wear my brother's hand-me-downs...

...he's a Saint Bernard.

I am the Oracle
of the
Winter Snow Blanket.

I see the mailman
through the
window of hope.

Oh. Hey there, Santa.
Sorry I ate all the cookies
Timmy left for you. But...
there's still plenty of milk!

Full disclosure:
Dairy doesn't agree with me.
It gives me gas.
But snickerdoodles, on the
other hand... (Sigh)
Well, like I said. Sorry about that.
#guilty

What kind of dog does
Ebenezer Scrooge have?

A bah hum-pug!

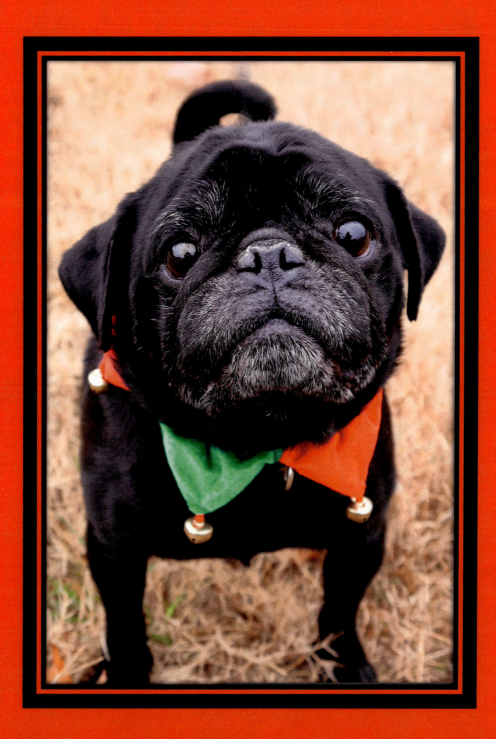

Hey Daddy-O.

Dig this... uh... I'm here for the Christmas Poetry Open Mic night. Catch my drift?

Let me lay out a beat for ya before I split this scene:

Santa's a square. In a round peg.
He don't fit. Like an Easter egg.
But I say Santa's a cool cat.
Meow.
Drop the mic now.

♫ Oh, the weather outside is frightful

But the fire is so delightful

And since we've no place to go

Let it Schnau, let it Schnau, let it Schnau! ♫

MAN'S BEST FRIEND

The kind of friend that helps man practice the ring-toss so he can win his girlfriend a giant teddy bear at the county fair.

Yeah, the mailman keeps putting
the old man's letters in my box.
I guess it's an honest mistake.
Our names kinda sound alike:
Santa Claus
Sandy Claws

If you see him before I do,
tell him Timmy wants a doll
and Suzy wants a dump truck.
Hmmm... pretty sure that's right.

Where's the RED bow tie?!

You can't fool me.

This is the same yellow bow
that went with my
Easter Bunny outfit!

I can't work in these conditions!

Okay, okay!

I'll wear the antlers!

Just as long as I don't have to

play with that stupid terrier.

Umm...

He's right behind me isn't he...

...awkward.

Yeah, yeah, I seen him.

Big fat guy driving a
sleigh with reindeer.

                    ...whatzit to you?

You found some fresh poop
under the Christmas tree?

Well, don't look at me.
I've been here all morning.

Yup. Just chewing on a bone.
All morning.
That's my story
and I'm sticking to it.

Feliz
Navi-dog!

WE THINK YOU'LL ALSO LIKE...

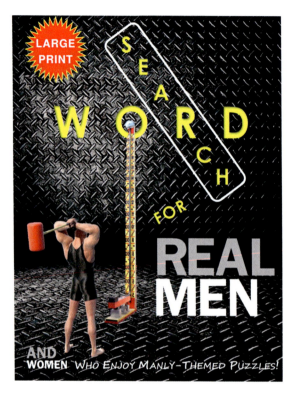

WORD SEARCH FOR REAL MEN
AND WOMEN WHO ENJOY MANLY-THEMED PUZZLES

DOWNLOAD FREE SAMPLE CHAPTERS AT:
www.fermtatahouse.com

Also from Fermata House…

ITCHY FEET TRAVEL TALES IN ASIA

Travel vicariously across the Orient with award-winning storyteller Sam Letchworth!

Sam savors every local culture he encounters much like Conan O'Brian and the late Anthony Bourdain — embracing the people, their food, and especially their curiosities. His humor and infatuation with humanity's diversity fuel each tale.

Teaching in Korea and Vietnam since 2015, Sam uses his time out of the classroom to explore the rest of Asia. His stories of the sublime and the surreal will have you giggling and gawking as you follow him through the weird and wonderful world of the East.

This short five-book series, *Itchy Feet Travel Tales in Asia*, covers Sam's adventures (and misadventures) in Cambodia, China, India, Indonesia, Japan, Korea, Malaysia, Mongolia, Myanmar, Russia, South Korea, Thailand, and Vietnam.

Book One: "Interrupting Cow"
Book Two: "Bambi Ate My Yen"
Book Three: "No Standing on Toilet"
Book Four: "Chew Tentacle Thoroughly"
Book Five: "You Like a Pho?"

What readers are saying:

"Irreverent in all the good ways."

"Mr. Letchworth possesses a rich comedic talent that makes his endearing stories even more delightful."

"All of his stories are either hysterical, heartwarming, fascinating, or some combination of all three."

"I love that the book includes photos."

"Put it on your coffee table or next to your commode and entertain guests with a quick story."

Fermata House
www.fermatahouse.com

"Happy Christmas to all,
and to all a good night!"